X 507.8
3525400
93y
Hopwood, James
Cool dry ice devices : fun
science projects with dry
ice

WITHDRAWN

APR 20

P9-DEK-840

Whitefish Bay Public Library

DATE DUE

OCT 2 8 2008			
AUG 3 0 2010			

FL-28-2

COOL
DRY ICE
DEVICES

Fun Science Projects with Dry Ice

James Hopwood

Whitefish Bay Public Library
5420 N. Marlborough Drive
Whitefish Bay, WI 53217

ABDO
Publishing Company

TO ADULT HELPERS

You're invited to assist an up-and-coming scientist! And it will pay off in many ways. Your children can develop new skills, gain confidence, and do some interesting projects while learning about science. What's more, it's going to be a lot of fun!

These projects are designed to let children work independently as much as possible. Encourage them to do whatever they are able to do on their own. Also encourage them to try the variations when supplied and to keep a science journal. Encourage children to think like real scientists.

Before getting started, set some ground rules about using the materials and ingredients. Most important, adult supervision is a must whenever a child uses the stove, chemicals, or dry ice.

So put on your lab coats and stand by. Let your young scientists take the lead. Watch and learn. Praise their efforts. Enjoy the scientific adventure!

VISIT US AT WWW.ABDOPUBLISHING.COM

Published by ABDO Publishing Company, 8000 West 78th Street, Edina, Minnesota 55439. Copyright © 2008 by Abdo Consulting Group, Inc. International copyrights reserved in all countries. No part of this book may be reproduced in any form without written permission from the publisher. The Checkerboard Library™ is a trademark and logo of ABDO Publishing Company.

Printed in the United States.

Design and Production: Mighty Media, Inc.
Art Direction: Kelly Doudna
Photo Credits: Kelly Doudna, iStockphoto/Maartje van Caspel, JupiterImages Corporation, Photodisc, Shutterstock
Series Editor: Pam Price
Consultant: Scott Devens

The following manufacturers/names appearing in this book are trademarks: C&H, DecoColor, Helix, Imperial, Land O Lakes, McCormick, Scotch, Sharpie, Sportline, Stanley, Workforce

Library of Congress Cataloging-in-Publication Data

Hopwood, James, 1964-
  Cool dry ice devices : fun science projects with dry ice / James Hopwood.
    p. cm. -- (Cool science)
  Includes index.
  ISBN 978-1-59928-907-6
  1. Dry ice--Experiments--Juvenile literature. 2. Science projects--Juvenile literature. 3. Science--Experiments--Juvenile literature. I. Title.

TP492.82.D78.H66 2008
507.8--dc22

2007010257

Contents

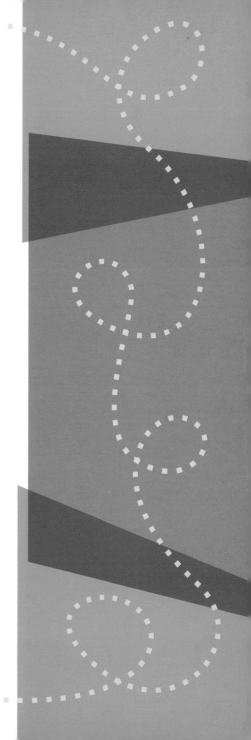

Science Is Cool..................... 4

The Scientific Method 6

Write It Down..................... 8

Safe Science 9

Cool Dry Ice Devices.............. 10

Materials 12

Hoppin' Poppers 14

Breezy Bubbles 16

Tasty Gassy Liquids............... 19

Fast Frozen Confections 22

Fantastic Fog Fountain 25

Sublime Sound Lens 28

Conclusion 30

Glossary 31

Web Sites.........................31

Index 32

Science Is Cool

Welcome to the cool world of science! Before we get started, let's put on our thinking caps. What do the following things have in common?

- bubbles in soda pop
- helium balloons that stay up in the air
- sounds you hear through the headphones of your music player
- a telescope that makes the faraway moon and stars appear closer
- choosing your right or left eye to look through a camera viewfinder
- your ability to balance on one foot

Did you guess that what they have in common is science? That's right, science! When you think of science, maybe you picture someone in a laboratory wearing a long white coat. Perhaps you imagine a scientist hunched over bubbling beakers and test tubes. But science is so much more. Let's take another look.

Soda pop doesn't develop bubbles until you open the container. That's because of a science called chemistry. Chemistry also explains why helium inside a balloon causes it to rise through the air.

You listen to your favorite song through the headphones attached to your music player. You look at the moon and stars through a telescope. Both activities are possible because of a science called physics. Did you know that eyeglasses improve your vision for the same reason telescopes work?

You tend to use the same eye each time you look through a camera viewfinder. You might find it challenging to balance on one foot. The science of biology helps explain why. Did you know it's related to the reason most people use only their left hand or right hand to write?

Broadly defined, science is the study of everything around us. Scientists use experiments and research to figure out how things work and relate to each other. The cool thing about science is that anyone can do it. You don't have to be a scientist in a laboratory to do science. You can do experiments with everyday things!

The Cool Science series introduces you to the world of science. Each book in this series will guide you through several simple experiments and projects with a common theme. The experiments use easy-to-find materials. Step-by-step instructions and photographs help guide your work.

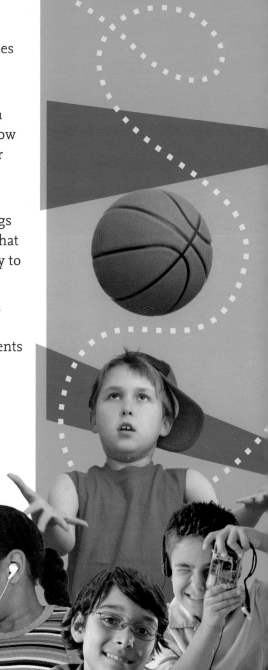

The Scientific Method

Scientists have a special way of working. It is called the scientific method. The scientific method is a series of steps that a scientist follows when trying to learn something. Following the steps makes it more likely that the information you discover will be reliable.

The scientific method is described on the next page. Follow all of the steps. These steps will help you learn the best information possible. And then you can draw an accurate conclusion about what happened. You will even write notes in your own science journal, just like real scientists do!

EVEN COOLER!

Check out sections like this one throughout the book. Here you'll find instructions for variations on the project. It might be a suggestion for a different way to do the project. Or it might be a similar project that uses slightly different materials. Either way, it will make your science project even cooler!

1. Observe

Simply pay attention to something. This is called observing. A good way to prepare for the next step is to make up a what, why, or how question about what you observe. For example, let's say you observe that when you open a bottle of soda pop and pour it into a glass, it gets bubbly. Your question could be, How do bubbles get into soda?

2. Hypothesize

Think of a statement that could explain what you have observed. This statement is called a hypothesis. You might remember that you also saw bubbles in your milk when you blew into it with a straw. So your hypothesis might be, I think somebody used a straw to blow into the soda before the bottle was sealed.

3. Test

Test your hypothesis. You do this by conducting an experiment. To test your hypothesis about how bubbles get into soda, you might mix up a recipe, blow into the liquid with a straw, quickly close the container, and then open it back up.

4. Conclude

Draw a conclusion. When you do this, you tie together everything that happened in the previous steps. You report whether the result of the experiment was what you hypothesized. Perhaps there were no bubbles in your soda pop recipe when you reopened the container. You would conclude that blowing through a straw is not how fizz gets into liquids.

Write It Down

A large part of what makes science science is observation. You should observe what happens as you work through an experiment. Scientists observe everything and write notes about it in journals. You can keep a science journal too. All you need is a notebook and a pencil.

At the beginning of each activity in this book, there is a section called "Think Like a Scientist." It contains suggestions about what to record in your science journal. You can predict what you think will happen. You can write down what did happen. And you can draw a conclusion, especially if what really happened is different from what you predicted.

As you do experiments, record things in your journal. You will be working just like a real scientist!

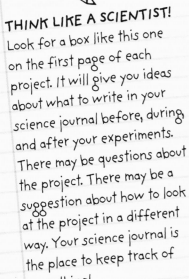

THINK LIKE A SCIENTIST!
Look for a box like this one on the first page of each project. It will give you ideas about what to write in your science journal before, during, and after your experiments. There may be questions about the project. There may be a suggestion about how to look at the project in a different way. Your science journal is the place to keep track of everything!

EVEN COOLER!
You can record more than just words in your journal. You can sketch pictures and make charts. If you have a camera, you can even add photos to your journal!

8

Safe Science

Good scientists practice safe science. Here are some important things to remember.

- Check with an adult before you begin any project. Sometimes you'll need an adult to buy materials or help you handle them for a while. For some projects, an adult will need to help you the whole time. The instructions will say when an adult should assist you.

- Ask for help if you're unsure about how to do something.

- If you or someone else is hurt, tell an adult immediately.

- Read the list of things you'll need. Gather everything before you begin working on a project.

- Don't taste, eat, or drink any of the materials or the results unless the directions say that you can.

- Use protective gear. Scientists wear safety goggles to protect their eyes. They wear gloves to protect their hands from chemicals and possible burns. They wear aprons or lab coats to protect their clothing.

- Clean up when you are finished. That includes putting away materials and washing containers, work surfaces, and your hands.

Cool Dry Ice Devices

Every day we see things that are hot and things that are cold. We know about solids, liquids, and gases. We see their relationship to each other illustrated when water freezes, melts, and **evaporates**. With the activities in this book, we'll go outside that range of everyday standards and explore the world of dry ice.

Dry ice is a common industrial product used in refrigerating, freezing, and preserving foods. And, in movies and stage shows, dry ice creates awesome fog.

Dry ice is created by compressing carbon dioxide gas (CO_2) until it turns into liquid. When the pressure is released, much of the CO_2 liquid suddenly evaporates back into a gas. But some of the liquid CO_2 freezes into a carbon dioxide "snow." The manufacturer collects that snow and compresses it into what we call dry ice.

So you see, dry ice is not made from water at all. In fact, it doesn't even melt like frozen water. In open air, dry ice turns back into a gas. That process is called **sublimation**. This happens because carbon dioxide can't be liquid at normal air pressure. That requires pressure five times greater than air pressure, so it changes directly to gas instead.

The name dry ice was created in the 1920s. The idea was to sell frozen carbon dioxide as an alternative to frozen water. Unlike water-based ice, dry ice doesn't melt and make a soggy mess. It also stays at a temperature of −109°F (−78°C)! So, it will keep food frozen until long after the dry ice is gone.

You can safely store dry ice in a cheap foam cooler. Wrapping the dry ice in newspaper helps preserve the solid form a little, but it will continue to sublimate. So buy it just before you plan to use it.

Dry Ice Safety

There are a few things to keep in mind when handling dry ice.

- The first is that −109°F is too cold to touch with bare skin. Dry ice can freeze your skin on contact. To keep your hands safe, always wear gloves when handling dry ice.

- Here's the second thing to remember. Always have plenty of ventilation when you work with dry ice. As it sublimates, dry ice gives off a lot of CO_2 gas that can make the air in a room unhealthy for breathing. CO_2 by itself is not harmful to breathe, but if it replaces the oxygen in an enclosed area, a hazardous situation could be created. If you ever feel dizzy when working with dry ice, simply get some fresh air right away and you will be okay.

- The third thing to remember is that dry ice is actually a highly compressed gas. Never store your dry ice in a sealed container. The gas will expand as it warms and cause a sealed container to explode.

Materials

You can probably find these supplies around the house.

gloves

35mm film canisters
(if your camera doesn't use film,
ask a local film processor to
save some canisters for you)

colored markers

spoon

stopwatch

tape measure
or ruler

bubble blower and
bubble solution

large kettle, bucket,
or drink cooler

cups

ladle

large mixing bowl

mixing spoon

old pillow case

small mixing bowl

permanent marker

serrated steak knife

duct tape

latex balloons

funnel

measuring spoons

measuring cups

AT THE GROCERY STORE
You can find these supplies at a grocery store.

sugar

cream

root beer extract

vanilla extract

foam cooler

AT THE HARDWARE STORE
You can find these supplies at a hardware store.

garbage can or large tub
with a loose lid or cover

mallet

AT THE DRY ICE STORE
Look in the phone book
for the nearest location.

dry ice crumbs

dry ice chips

dryer hose

dry ice blocks

13

Hoppin' Poppers

TIME: ABOUT 15 MINUTES

MATERIALS

35mm film canisters

paint pens or colored markers

gloves

dry ice chips

spoon

stopwatch

tape measure or ruler

Discover how much gas is in a solid, and vice versa.

CHEMISTRY

THINK LIKE A SCIENTIST!

Try some variations on the experiment. Put the canisters upside down. Add some water to the dry ice before closing the canisters. But don't switch to harder containers that could be dangerous. Compare your results as you answer these questions.

1. Which film canisters work the best? Why do you think that is?
2. How do different amounts of dry ice change the results?
3. How does adding water to the canister affect the pop?
4. How does the pop change if the canisters are upside down?

1. Use a paint pen or marker to put matching names, numbers, or pictures on the lids and sides of the film canisters.

2. Use the spoon to put a small amount of dry ice in each container.

3. Seal the matching lids back onto the canisters. Quickly set them upright on a level surface and step back.

4. In a few moments, the lids will pop off the canisters. Record how long they take to pop and how high they go.

5. Do the experiment again using different kinds of film canisters and different amounts of dry ice. See if you can determine which combinations pop highest or fastest.

The Science behind the Fun

Dry ice is basically a frozen gas. Unlike liquids, which freeze and melt at close to the same volume, gases don't have a set volume. Gases expand to fill any container they are in. Adding more gas raises the pressure, but the container determines the volume.

This experiment shows exactly why you should never put dry ice in a sealed container. Film canisters are small, soft, and pop open when the gas expands. A fully sealed, hard container could explode dangerously into many sharp, flying pieces. Seriously, don't try it.

Science at Work

Class B fire extinguishers are filled with CO_2, but the sealed containers don't burst. That's because extinguisher tanks are built to hold high pressure. If you look at the gauge on a CO_2 fire extinguisher, you'll see that the pressure is around 200 pounds per square inch (14 kg/sq cm)! That's the same as a 200-pound man standing on your big toe!

Breezy Bubbles

TIME: ABOUT 50 MINUTES

MATERIALS

garbage can or large tub with a loose lid or cover

gloves

about a pound (0.5 kg) dry ice

bubble blower and bubble solution

Which is heavier, CO_2 gas or the air around you? You'll find out with this activity.

CHEMISTRY

THINK LIKE A SCIENTIST!

Answer these questions in your science journal.

1. What did you expect to happen?
2. What actually did happen?
3. Would an air-filled balloon float as well as the soap bubbles?

1. Place the dry ice in the bottom of the tub and close the lid loosely. Let the dry ice **sublimate** into gas until the solid is mostly gone. After about 45 minutes, check inside the tub. Lift the lid very slowly so you don't stir up the gas.

2. Once the dry ice is almost gone, remove the lid carefully. Can you see pooled CO_2 gas in the bottom of the tub?

3. Use the bubble wand to blow bubbles over the top of the tub so they will fall down into the gas. Don't blow down into the barrel because that would stir up the CO_2.

4. Watch what happens when the bubbles hit the pool of gas. Now add a little cold water to the bottom of the tub to speed up the sublimation of the remaining dry ice. Then repeat step 3.

EVEN COOLER!

Put two cubic inches (33 cc, an amount that's about the size of your fist) of dry ice into an empty pitcher. Cover the pitcher with a paper towel to keep the gas in. When the dry ice has sublimated away, pour the gas from the pitcher over a candle flame.

The Science behind the Fun

CO_2 gas is about one and one-half times heavier than air. That's why it collects in the bottom of the tub instead of floating out. If it weren't contained, the gas would settle to the floor. There it would spread like a big, slow-moving puddle of water.

Soap bubbles weigh only as much as the soap and water it takes to make them. Outdoors, they float only because a light breeze moves them. However, an air-filled bubble will float on the CO_2.

Science at Work

Dangerous gases such as natural gas or carbon monoxide are invisible. They are heavier than air, so they fall to the floor in calm air. Natural gas from a leak can run along the floor until a spark **ignites** it. Then the whole cloud of gas can burst into flame.

If carbon monoxide leaks from a broken furnace or water heater, it can build up on the floor. Breathing carbon monoxide lowers your blood's ability to gather oxygen from the air. Too much exposure can cause suffocation. If you are exposed to carbon monoxide gas, move to fresh air and call 911.

Tasty Gassy Liquids

TIME: ABOUT 60 MINUTES

MATERIALS

4-gallon (15 L) kettle, bucket, or insulated drink cooler

1½ gallons (6 L) cool drinking water

3 cups (0.6 kg) sugar

1½ ounces (44 ml) root beer extract or vanilla extract

gloves

2 pounds (0.9 kg) dry ice

ladle

several thirsty friends with cups

Some might say that the best part about carbon dioxide is how it stings your nose. Some say it's sort of like a good root beer burp. Let's put that theory to the test.

Important safety note! Never use solid dry ice to cool your beverage. It could cause injury if you swallow it. Use only ice cubes made with water.

CHEMISTRY

McCormick.
Root Beer Concentrate

INGREDIENTS: CARAMEL COLOR, WATER, CORN SYRUP, WILD CHERRY BARK EXTRACTIVES AND OTHER NATURAL EXTRACTIVES, NATURAL AND ARTIFICIAL FLAVORS, METHYL SALICYLATE (FLAVORING AGENT), VANILLIN, GUM ARABIC, GUM TRAGACANTH, AND SULFITING AGENTS.
McCORMICK & CO., INC.
HUNT VALLEY, MD 21031-1100
PACKED IN U.S.A.

NET 2 FL OZ 59 mL

THINK LIKE A SCIENTIST!
Answer these questions in your science journal.

1. Is the root beer as fizzy as you thought it would be?
2. How long did the fizz last?
3. Do you think adding more dry ice would give it more fizz?
4. Who had the best root beer burp?

1 Put the sugar and the water into the container. Stir until the sugar dissolves. Then add the root beer extract and stir it in. If you prefer cream soda, use vanilla extract instead.

2 Taste your mixture. If you think it needs more flavoring or sugar, now is the time to add it.

3 Carefully add the dry ice to the mixture. Cover with a loose lid if desired. Remember to not seal the container completely, or it might burst.

4 After one hour, all the dry ice should be sublimated and the root beer ready to serve. Look closely and be careful not to serve any dry ice in the drinking cups. It may seem exciting to have a foggy cup, but contact with the dry ice might burn you or your guests.

5 Test your root beer for fizz and burpability.

TIP
Make sure your container holds at least twice as much liquid as the amount of water you're using. That way, your root beer will have room to bubble after you add the dry ice. And, you won't have a big mess to clean up later!

The Science behind the Fun

A lot happens when you put dry ice in water. The water speeds up the sublimation, so the dry ice releases a lot of gas under the water. Next, the extremely cold gas chills the water vapor inside the bubbles. This makes the vapor **condense** into the microscopic droplets we call fog. Then the cold, dense fog pours over the sides of the container.

The fog cloud fades away as the water droplets warm up and **evaporate** again. In the meantime, some CO_2 dissolves into the water. The CO_2 stays dissolved in water as long as it stays cold and under pressure. If not, the CO_2 bubbles right back out as fizz.

Science at Work

CO_2 dissolves into water faster at high pressure and lower temperature. Soda manufacturers mix compressed CO_2 with water inside high-pressure tanks to speed up the process. This also produces a higher level of carbonation. The tanks they use operate at pressures up to 200 pounds per square inch (14 kg/sq cm). You can't reach those pressures safely at home without special equipment.

⭐

EVEN COOLER!

Make a simple low-pressure system to increase the fizz factor. Get a five-gallon (19 L) frosting container with a two-inch (5 cm) pour spout from your local bakery. Clean the bucket thoroughly before using it. Remove the cap from the pour spout before you start. Mix your root beer in the bucket and add the dry ice. Seal the lid onto the bucket with the pour spout open. Cover the spout opening with a smooth three-pound (1.4 k) weight to make a pressure-release **valve**. Pressure inside the bucket will lift the weight and escape without popping off the lid. Let the root beer brew for an hour. Remove the lid and use a ladle to serve the root beer.

Fast Frozen Confections

TIME: ABOUT 45 MINUTES

You know that dry ice is cold. But how cold is it, and can it make dessert?

CHEMISTRY

MATERIALS

4 cups (1 L) cream

¾ cup (150 g) sugar

2 teaspoons (10 ml) vanilla

large mixing bowl

sturdy mixing spoon

gloves

2 pounds (0.9 kg) dry ice

old pillow case

mallet

small mixing bowl

THINK LIKE A SCIENTIST!

Answer these questions in your science journal.

1. Did the experiment work as quickly as you expected?

2. Do you think there are better ways to crush the ice?

3. Are there more exciting ice-cream recipes to freeze?

4. Do you like **sorbet**?

1 Mix together the cream, sugar, and vanilla in the large mixing bowl.

2 Place half of the dry ice in the pillowcase and crush it with a mallet until it's powder and crumbs. Pour the **pulverized** dry ice into the small mixing bowl. Repeat this with the rest of the dry ice.

3 Stir the cream mixture constantly and slowly spoon in the dry ice. Don't add too much dry ice at once, or the cream will foam out of the bowl. When the mixture becomes thicker, slow down adding the dry ice. If you add too much dry ice, your ice cream will become rock hard.

4 When the mixture becomes too thick to stir, stop adding dry ice. Place the ice cream in a freezer or a cooler.

5 Check the ice cream after about an hour to make sure all of the dry ice has completely **sublimated**. As soon as the dry ice is gone, the ice cream is safe to eat.

EVEN COOLER!

Cover some fresh strawberries in dry ice powder to **flash freeze** them. Put them and some unfrozen strawberries into the freezer overnight. In the morning, let the strawberries thaw. Then compare the taste and texture of the berries. Does flash freezing with dry ice give a fresher-tasting result than the traditional freezing method? Write your observations in your science journal.

The Science behind the Fun

When two things with different temperatures come into contact, they share energy and eventually become the same temperature. The dry ice started out at -109°F (-78°C). The cream mixture was probably around 40°F (4°C).

The dry ice pulled heat from the cream mixture. That froze the water in the cream. At the same time, the heat from the cream raised the temperature of the dry ice above its freezing point. As a result, the ice cream froze and the dry ice turned back into gas, leaving a slightly carbonated result.

Science at Work

The extremely cold temperature of dry ice makes it perfect for keeping things frozen. It is used for extended storage when electric refrigeration isn't available. When some people go camping, they use a second cooler full of dry ice along with a cooler full of food. That way they can keep food frozen on long trips. And, they do not need to head into town every couple of days to buy more ice.

Fantastic Fog Fountain

TIME: ABOUT 30 MINUTES

Whenever you see dry ice, there is at least a little bit of fog around it. In this activity you will make a simple fog machine that will make an awesome amount of fog.

MATERIALS

foam cooler

4 feet (1 m) dryer hose

permanent marker

serrated steak knife

duct tape

2 gallons (8 L) hot water

gloves

1½ pounds (0.7 kg) dry ice

CHEMISTRY

THINK LIKE A SCIENTIST!

Answer these questions in your science journal.

1. How long did the fog last?
2. Why did the fog stop?
3. If you were to do this again, what would you do differently?
4. How could you get different results if you wanted more fog or less fog?

1 Place an end of the dryer hose against the center of the cooler lid. Trace its outline onto the lid with the marker.

2 Use the steak knife to cut a hole through the lid. Carefully follow the inside of the line you traced. The hose should fit snugly in this hole, so be careful not to cut it too large.

3 Push one end of the dryer hose into the hole. Seal the connection with duct tape. You will probably yank on this tape joint, so make it strong!

Science at Work

Photographers and movie makers use dry ice to create fog effects. The fog lies on the ground like a blanket. This effect lends a scary and unreal touch to a scene. Musicians and magicians sometimes use fog machines to fill the stage with fog.

4 Make sure the lid is nearby. Then pour the hot water into the bottom of the cooler.

5 Carefully and quickly drop the dry ice into the hot water and close the lid. You may want to tape the lid to keep it in place.

6 Use the hose to direct the fog stream to where you want it.

The Science behind the Fun

The heat of the water **sublimates** the dry ice at a much faster rate than cold water can. However, the extreme cold of the escaping CO_2 gas chills the water vapor into a thick fog. When the dry ice and the water exchange energy, they combine to become a cloud of CO_2 gas and water mist. The mist will settle to the floor if it's left alone, giving you a nice puffy fog.

Sublime Sound Lens

TIME: ABOUT 25 MINUTES

MATERIALS

9-inch (23 cm) latex balloons

gloves

crumbs of dry ice

funnel or folded paper

measuring spoons

CHEMISTRY

This is a fun trick to do with some spare dry ice.

THINK LIKE A SCIENTIST!

Record your observations in your science journal.

1. What did you hear?
2. Could you hear whispers better through the balloon?
3. Does the balloon need to be positioned just right for this to work?
4. Does the inflated balloon seem heavier than a normal balloon?

1 Insert the funnel into the opening of a balloon. Use thicker, helium-quality balloons if they are available.

2 Use a measuring spoon to put about 1 tablespoon (15 cc) of dry ice crumbs into the balloon.

3 Remove the funnel and tie a knot in the balloon, as if it were inflated.

4 Let the dry ice **sublimate** to fill the balloon. If the balloon pops, use a little less dry ice in the next one. If it doesn't inflate entirely, use a little more dry ice in the next one.

5 Once the dry ice has completely sublimated, hold the filled balloon near your ear. Listen to faint and distant sounds through it. Do not do this if the dry ice is still sublimating to inflate the balloon. Having a balloon pop near your ear is never fun and can cause deafness.

The Science behind the Fun

Sound doesn't move as quickly through CO_2 as it does through air. So, the balloon acts like a lens for sound, much like curved glass acts as a lens for light. The balloon gathers sound and focuses it to your ear. This is similar to the way a magnifying lens focuses sunlight to burn paper.

Science at Work

Marine biologists are studying the large foreheads of dolphins. They are calling the foreheads "acoustic windows." The biologists' theory is that these sound lenses help focus the high-pitched tones dolphins use for **echolocation**.

Conclusion

As you have seen, dry ice doesn't act like anything you come across on a daily basis! It's quite an eye-opener to see how lowering the temperature changes everything. The extreme temperature and unusual states of matter make dry ice both difficult and useful to work with.

There are even stranger materials out there that make dry ice seem ordinary. For example, liquid nitrogen boils at −320°F (−196°C). If you were to drop a piece of dry ice into it, the heat of the dry ice would make the liquid nitrogen boil. Liquid helium boils at −452°F (−269°C). That's barely warmer than absolute zero. That's the coldest anything can be!

Science brings us new materials and properties that don't exist in nature. We then manufacture those materials and use their unique properties to make our lives easier. That's why we should keep looking beyond what we see in front of us. That's how we can discover things we weren't even looking for!

Glossary

condense – to cause a gas to change to a liquid or a solid form.

echolocation – a process for locating distant or unseen objects by using sound waves.

evaporate – to change from a liquid or a solid into a vapor.

flash freeze – to freeze rapidly.

ignite – to set on fire.

pulverize – to beat, grind, or smash something into powder or dust.

sorbet – a fruit-flavored ice.

sublimate – to change from a solid to a gaseous form without changing into a liquid form.

valve – a mechanical device that controls the flow of gas, liquids, or other materials.

WEB SITES

To learn more about dry ice, visit ABDO Publishing Company on the World Wide Web at **www.abdopublishing.com.** Web sites about dry ice are featured on our Book Links page. These links are routinely monitored and updated to provide the most current information available.

Index

A

Adult help (for safety), 9

B

Balloon experiment, 28–29
Biology, 5
Bubble experiment, 16–18

C

Canister experiment, 14–15
Carbon dioxide, 10, 11, 15,
    17–19, 21, 27, 29
    See also Dry ice
Carbon monoxide, 18
Chemistry, 4
Cleaning up, 9
Conclusion (and scientific
    method), 6, 7, 8
Condensation, 21

D

Dangerous gases, 18
Dolphins, 29
Drink experiment, 19–21.
    See also Eating/Drinking
Dry ice
    qualities of, 10–11
    safety guidelines for, 11,
    15, 18, 19, 20, 21, 23, 29
    storage of, 11

E

Eating/Drinking (of
    science materials), 9, 19,
    20, 21, 23, 24
Echolocation, 29

Evaporation, 10, 21
Expansion (of dry ice), 11,
    14–15, 21
Explosions (caused by dry
    ice), 15

F

Fire extinguishers, 15
Flash freezing, 24
Fog (creation of), 21, 25–27

H

Hypothesis (and scientific
    method), 7

I

Ice cream experiment,
    22–24
Injuries, 9

L

Liquid nitrogen, 30

M

Magicians, 26
Marine biologists, 29
Materials (gathering/
    putting away of), 9,
    12–13
Movies, 26
Musicians, 26

N

Natural gas, 18

O

Observation (and scientific
    method), 7

P

Photographers, 26
Physics, 4–5
Protective gear, 9, 11

R

Refrigeration, 24
Root beer experiment,
    19–21

S

Safety guidelines, 9, 11, 15,
    18, 19, 20, 21, 23, 29
Science
    definition of, 4–5, 30
    materials for, 9, 12–13
    method for, 6–7
    safety guidelines for, 9.
    See also Safety guidelines
    writing about, 6, 8
Science journals, 6, 8
Scientific method, 6–7
Soda pop, 7, 21
Sorbet experiment, 22–24
Sublimation, 10, 17, 21, 23,
    27, 29

T

Testing (and scientific
    method), 7

V

Ventilation, 11